Teaching the Stories and Poems of Edgar Allan Poe

By Tara McCarthy

New York • Toronto • London • Auckland • Sydney
Mexico City • New Delhi • Hong Kong

Scholastic Inc. grants teachers permission to photocopy the reproducible pages from this book for classroom use. No other part of this publication may be reproduced in whole or in part, or stored in a retrieval system, or transmitted in any form or by any means, electronic, mechanical, photocopying, recording, or otherwise, without permission of the publisher. For information regarding permission, write to Scholastic Professional Books, 555 Broadway, New York, NY 10012.

Cover design by Jaime Lucero and Norma Ortiz
Interior design by Drew Hires
Interior illustrations by Drew Hires
Poster design by Drew Hires

Copyright © 1999 by Tara McCarthy. All rights reserved.
ISBN 0-590-66138-8
Printed in the U.S.A.

Contents

INTRODUCTION 5
   How the Stories and Poems Are Presented 5
   General Hints 6
   Additional Resources: Books, Audiotapes, and Web Sites 7

EDGAR ALLAN POE: A BRIEF BIOGRAPHY 8

STUDYING A STORY TOGETHER 11
   "The Fall of the House of Usher" 11
   Synopsis; Teaching Notes 11
   Prereading Activities 12
   While Reading: Comprehension Questions 13
   Follow-up Activities: Reading and Writing 13
   Curriculum Connections 15
      ART, MUSIC, MEDIA, TECHNOLOGY
   REPRODUCIBLES: Tracking the Story 16
                   Planning a Poe-like Story 17

READERS THEATER 18
   "The Masque of the Red Death" 18
   Synopsis; Teaching Notes 18
   Prereading/Acting Activities 19
   Preparing and Presenting the Play 20
   Curriculum Connections 21
      ART/WRITING, LITERARY ANALYSIS,
      MUSIC, HEALTH/SCIENCE
   REPRODUCIBLES: Play Script 22
                   A Letter to Poe 26

GROUP WORK 27
   "Ligeia," "Hop-Frog," and "The Tell-Tale Heart" 27
   Synopses; Teaching Notes 27
   Prereading Activities 28
   Follow-up Activities: Discussing and Writing 29
   REPRODUCIBLES: Reading Circle Cards 30
                   Literary Elements in Poe's Stories 33

READERS THEATER 34
"The Purloined Letter" 34
Synopsis; Teaching Notes 34
Prereading/Acting Activities 35
Preparing and Presenting the Play 35
Curriculum Connections 36
CAREER SKILLS, CRITICAL VIEWING, TECHNOLOGY/SCIENCE, WRITING, CIVICS/HISTORY, VISUAL SKILLS, ART, GAMES, AN ANTHOLOGY
Bringing the Stories Together 37
REPRODUCIBLES: Play Script 40
               The Elements of a Plot 48
               Planning a Mystery Story 49

FOUR POEMS BY EDGAR ALLAN POE TO READ TOGETHER 50
"The Raven" 50
Synopsis 50
Teaching Notes; Follow-up 51
REPRODUCIBLES: "The Raven," arranged for choral reading 52
               Exploring Poe Sounds 59
               Writing a Poe-like Poem 60

"Eldorado" and "Annabel Lee" 61
Synopses 61
Teaching Notes; Follow-up 62
REPRODUCIBLES: "Eldorado" 63
               "Annabel Lee" 65
               Meet You at the Movies 67

"The Bells" 68
Synopsis; Teaching Notes 68
Follow-up 69
REPRODUCIBLES: "The Bells," arranged for choral reading 70
               Using Poe's Techniques in Your Poems 74

POE'S STORIES AND POEMS: CULMINATING ACTIVITIES 75
REPRODUCIBLE: Poe's Wonderful Words: An Annotated Glossary 77

POSTER .... (bound in back)

Introduction

The stories and poems of Edgar Allan Poe are both easy and challenging to use in the classroom. Easy, because tales and narrative poems that deal with mystery, horror, and suspense greatly appeal to most young people today. Challenging, because the works are written in the dramatic, dense language typical of Poe and most of his contemporaries. Yet teachers report that students of widely varying reading abilities all happily tackle the language because they're rewarded with the amazing tales that Poe's words weave.

This book aims to help your students enjoy the challenges in order to get to know the work of one of America's most influential writers. Poe was the originator of the modern detective story, and also, through his "terror tales" and soulful poems, a master at the following: establishing a *setting*, sustaining an *atmosphere*, creating unforgettable *characters*, building an intriguing *plot*, and developing powerful *themes* dealing with love, loss, courage, greed, fear, and the search for one's heart's desire. Thus, Poe's work presents in bold strokes the literary elements that you want your students to identify as they read modern stories and emulate in their own story writing.

How the Stories and Poems Are Presented
- The first story, "The Fall of the House of Usher," is presented for the whole class to study together, as an introduction to Poe's work.
- Three stories—"Ligeia," "Hop-Frog," and "The Tell-Tale Heart"—are presented for small-group study and follow-up class sharing and discussion.
- Two stories —"The Masque of the Red Death" and "The Purloined Letter"—are presented in readers theater form.
- Four of Poe's poems are presented in full, with two arranged for choral reading.

Accompanying the Stories and Poems You'll Find:
- Synopses
- Suggestions for prereading activities
- While-reading prompts, suggestions, and activities

- After-reading activities that focus on:
  - whole-class discussions
  - literary elements
  - vocabulary development
  - applying reading to writing
  - curriculum connections
  - independent, partner, and group projects
  - activities and reproducibles for students with different learning styles

Poster

Display the poster at the start of your Poe unit. Encourage students to refer to it as they read the biographical information on pages 8–10.

General Hints

1. A Cautionary Note

As you may be aware, Poe's stories often deal with characters who have lifestyles or habits that parents in your community may not even want to have *mentioned* in the classroom! For example, in "Ligeia," the narrator muses briefly over his addiction to opium. To avoid possible hassles from families at home, consider one or both of the following strategies: 1) Always read or listen to a tape recording of the story ahead of time. Decide which parts it may be advisable for you to skip over or reword when presenting the story to your students. 2) Be up front. Tell students ahead of time that one of the reasons some of Poe's characters meet an untimely end is because they have addictions or habits that impair their reasoning. You can set this in a historical context if you wish. Tell students that people in Poe's day were not as aware as we are now of how drugs make people unable to behave in sensible ways.

2. Take Your Time and Do Things Your Way

- *If you're reading the story aloud to the class*, read the story in parts, over a period of two or three days. Feel free to leave out or summarize sections that you think may be too difficult or too repetitive for your students to attend to. Call on students to recap the narrative before you go on to the next part.

- *Make your own tape recording of the story for kids to listen to.* You may want to leave out or summarize certain sections before resuming with Poe's paragraphs.

- *If you've asked student groups to listen to commercial tape-recorded tellings of a story*, encourage them to stop the tape occasionally to review what's happened so far, to ask and answer questions, to predict what will happen next, and to briefly discuss their reactions to the story.

- *Enjoy your role as mentor and most-experienced reader!* Students learn a lot when the teacher shares with them his or her gut responses to any story or poem. What words, phrases, images, and ideas particularly impress you? By briefly and enthusiastically sharing your own reactions and impressions, you not only provide models for students to follow in their independent discussions, but also demonstrate the universal appeal of Poe's work.

Additional Resources

BOOKS
For Students:
- Avi's *The Man Who Was Poe* is a fine, definitive biography.

- From Scholastic:
    - *Eight Tales of Terror* (ISBN 00590411365)
    - *The Great Mysteries* by Edgar Allan Poe (ISBN 059043344X)
    - *The Raven and Other Poems* (ISBN 05900452606)

For You, the Teacher
- *Poe: A Biography*, by William Bittner (Little, Brown). The epilogue and the author's follow-up, "The Poe Controversies," are especially valuable for summaries on how the facts of Poe's life contrast with the myths and disparaging reports that followed his death.

- *Edgar Allan Poe: Sixty-Seven Tales* (Gramercy Books). This inexpensive hardcover also includes Poe's only novel (*The Narrative of Arthur Gordon Pym*) and 31 of his poems.

AUDIOTAPES
- Listen and Read: "The Raven" and Other Poems (ISBN 04864001308)
- Edgar Allan Poe's "The Tell-Tale Heart" and Other Stories (ISBN 0486291235)
- The Best of Poe Read Along (ISBN 0785407421)
- Classic Poe (ISBN 1883049393)
- National Public Radio has a great tape-recorded reading of "The Tell-Tale Heart." Call 202-414-3232 for ordering information.

WEB SITES FOR MYSTERY LOVERS
- LITERARY LOCALES (www.sjsu.edu/depts/english). On this page, maintained by the Department of English at San Jose State University, students can click "Edgar Allan Poe's Favorite Haunts." There they'll find links to Poe's homes in the Bronx and in Baltimore, to the Poe museum in Richmond, and—under "A Poe Pourri"—samples of his work and a brief biography.

- ONLINE MYSTERY DATABASE (http://www.aetv.com/mystery). The sponsor is A&E Television Networks. It's a good resource for students who want to explore favorite mystery writers, characters, novels, films, and TV shows.

- SCHOLASTIC PLACE: BOOKS AND BOOK CLUBS (http://scholastic.com/). The sponsor is Scholastic Inc. Kids can get information regarding popular mystery and adventure series published by Scholastic (e.g., "Babysitters Club," "Goosebumps," "Animorphs") and updates about TV programs and videos related to them.

Edgar Allan Poe
A Brief Biography

The Early Years

Edgar Allan Poe was born on January 19, 1809, in Boston, Massachusetts. His parents were itinerant actors, and often down on their luck. Poe's father deserted the family early on, and his mother died when he was just three years old.

Poe was immediately taken in by Frances (a friend of his mother) and John Allan (which is how Poe got his middle name) of Richmond, Virginia, who raised him lovingly—especially Mrs. Allan, who doted on the boy and whom Poe called "Mama." John Allan was a Scottish self-made merchant. He sent Edgar to the best schools in Richmond, and then to fine schools in England for several years while Mr. Allan was there on business. From all accounts, young Poe was a model scholar and a popular leader among his schoolmates.

Edgar Allan Poe
(1809 – 1849)

Growing Up

By 1820, back in Richmond and moving into his teenage years, Poe was exhibiting some of the traits that would eventually make him a great writer: a liking for reciting poetry aloud; a tendency to take risks (like swimming six miles against the tide across the James River); a habit of constantly falling into daydreams and romantic pining; and a distinct aversion to following his foster father's footsteps into the worlds of business and law.

As a result, Poe and John Allan fell into an on-again, off-again affection. Allan feared the boy was ungrateful and not serious enough, so he cut off Poe's tuition payments during Poe's first year at the University of Virginia. Allan then complained when Poe began to gamble to earn school fees. In an attempt to both please Allan and to break away from him, Poe served two years in the army, then enrolled in the U.S. Military Academy at West Point. But when Frances Allan died in 1829 and John Allan quickly remarried, all funds for support were cut off. The breach was final, and Poe was on his own.

Becoming a Professional Writer

By the time Poe was 21 years old, two of his volumes of poetry had been published. The books sold poorly, however. Desperate for money, Poe tried his hand at short stories, and in 1833 found fame and a $50 prize (big money then!) with "MS. Found in a Bottle." Editors and fellow writers began to find Poe's work compelling—not only his stories and poems but also his astute literary criticisms and editing abilities. As an editor, Poe worked on literary magazines in Philadelphia and New York City, writing stories and poems at the same time.

By 1845, Poe had achieved as much fame and recognition as he would ever have in his lifetime. His story "The Gold Bug" sold 300,000 copies; the poem "The Raven" became an instant success; and the esteemed writer James Russell Lowell declared Poe "the most discriminating, philosophical, and fearless critic upon imaginative works who has ever written in America."

It was in his work as a literary critic that Poe, unknowingly, made a lifelong enemy: he gave a lukewarm review to the works of Rufus Wilmot Griswold. In the ensuing years, Griswold pretended that Poe's reviews did not bother him, and indeed proclaimed to be Poe's earnest friend. Time would show otherwise.

Personal Life

Poe was always yearning for home and family, and found them with his devoted aunt, Maria Clemm (his father's sister), and her daughter—Poe's cousin—Virginia. In 1836, Poe and Virginia married. For Poe, Maria Clemm was the mother he had always wanted, and Virginia was the frail yet steadfast woman he celebrated in many of his poems and stories. The threesome wandered from city to city, always impoverished by Poe's tendency to run up debts. They finally settled in New York City, where, in 1847, after five years of illness, Virginia died of tuberculosis.

At about this time, Poe began to tell friends that he sensed his own death was near. To prepare, he asked Rufus Griswold to be the executor of his estate, and Griswold agreed.

The Final Days

In 1849, Poe—now living in Richmond—became engaged to a childhood sweetheart, Sarah Royster Shelton. He set northward by train on September 27 to fetch his beloved aunt, Mrs. Clemm, so that he could accompany her back south to the wedding.

The train stopped in Baltimore on September 28 or 29. Poe debarked, and supposedly went to visit friends, who were not at home. Then came the "lost days." It has never been established what happened to Poe in those final four days. On October 3, he was found, half conscious, in a doorway. He was rushed to a hospital, but could not be revived. He died on October 7, 1849.

Poe's Reputation

Poe was known in his lifetime for being constantly in debt and for telling lies in order to get money out of friends and sympathizers, who seemed willing nonetheless to subsidize him as he worked 18 hours a day to turn out admirable stories, poems, and literary critiques. Basically, Poe was known as a gifted, hardworking, but n'er-do-well writer, always living on the edge. Poe's posthumous reputation as a drug addict and alcoholic was created by Rufus Griswold, whom Poe had naively named executor of his literary estate. Griswold, finally revenging himself for Poe's lukewarm reviews in years past, wrote letters, obituaries, and columns stating that Poe was a degenerate; he tossed overboard from a ferryboat some of Poe's last works and letters. Griswold's view of Poe has managed to survive through the years. Recently, however, scholars have agreed—based on analyses of records of Poe's final hospital stay and on Poe's own statements and dire premonitions a year before his death—that Poe, who seldom drank because he was allergic to alcohol, probably died from diabetes or a brain tumor.

Whatever the truth about Poe's personal habits, the man remains—through his work—the inventor of the detective story, the critic who set standards for evaluating literature, the poet who captured mood through rhyme and rhythm, and the story writer who dared to delve into the deepest recesses of our dreams.

Studying a Story Together
"The Fall of the House of Usher"

Synopsis

The first-person narrator ("I") goes to visit Roderick Usher, a childhood friend whom he has not seen since school days. The gloomy, decaying atmosphere of the mansion matches the strange moods and behavior of Roderick, who—with his twin sister, Madeline—is the last of the long, noble family (house) of Usher. Roderick suffers from a heightening of his senses—especially of his sense of hearing—and is grieving over Madeline, who is dying from a mysterious illness. The narrator tries in vain to bolster his friend's spirits.

Madeline dies, and the narrator assists Roderick in burying her in the family vault in the cellar. Roderick's behavior becomes increasingly odd. A week after Madeline's burial, while the narrator is reading a story to Roderick in an attempt to distract him, fearsome sounds—creaking, ripping, clanging—echo through the house. Roderick declares he has been hearing such sounds ever since his sister was entombed, and shrieks,"I tell you that she now stands without [outside] the door!"

Sure enough, Madeline—bloody from the effort of escaping her tomb—appears in the doorway. Dying at last, she falls upon her brother, who dies, too, from shock. Just as the terrified narrator escapes from the decaying house, he sees it break apart, crumble entirely, and sink into the lake.

Teaching Notes

1. This story achieves what Poe considered to be the highest standard for a literary work: a unity of effect or impression. Poe carefully chose words to create images that build an atmosphere of increasing doom, gloom, mental instability, and terror. Nothing in the story distracts from this unity.

2. How did Madeline Usher get out of that tomb? She wasn't really dead! Hints in the story suggest that she had an illness that was accompanied by *catalepsy*—a physical state in which all bodily functions seem to have stopped. Nowadays, of course, medical science can distinguish catalepsy from death. But in Poe's day, doctors didn't always know the difference. Therefore, the story builds on the general fear in those times of premature burial, that is, that one might actually be buried alive.

3. The story title incorporates the two meanings of the term "house of." It can mean a literal building; or, in olden days, "house of" also meant family, especially a noble family like the Ushers. In Poe's story, the collapse (fall) of the building also symbolizes the end (fall) of the family, since Roderick and Madeline were its last surviving members.

Prereading Activities

Use Prior Knowledge
Invite students to tell about the following:
- A huge vacant house or other dilapidated building that seemed "scary" to them. What made it scary? What did they imagine might be inside? What kept them from entering the house, or challenged them to enter it after all?

- A visit to a friend not seen in a long, long time. How had the friend changed? How was she or he just the same?

Choose a Mode of Presentation
On page 6, you'll find suggestions for different ways of presenting the story to your students.

Focus on Literary Elements
- **Plot:** If necessary, review that *plot* is the series of events that take place in a story. Explain that "The Fall of the House of Usher" tells about the strange events the narrator encounters when visiting the home of an old friend.

- **Atmosphere:** Introduce or review the term *atmosphere*: the general feeling or mood in a story. Atmosphere can usually be summarized in a word or brief phrase, e.g., a funny story, a mysterious adventure, a scary situation. You may wish to have students identify the atmosphere in various stories or chapters of books they've recently read. Read aloud teaching note 1 on page 11 to stress that Poe was very big on establishing atmosphere.

- **Setting:** *Setting* is where a story takes place. Mention that Poe set most of his stories in gloomy houses, dungeons, and mysterious castles. Suggest to students that they write down—as they read or hear "The Fall of the House of Usher"—their own words and phrases to describe the story atmosphere and setting.

Set Goals

Distribute the reproducible on page 16 (Tracking the Story). Preview with students what the activity requires them to do. Suggest that students work with a reading or listening partner to complete the page as they enjoy the story.

While Reading: Comprehension Questions

If students are hearing the story read aloud by you or on tape, pause to ask the following questions for class discussion. If students are reading or listening independently or in small groups, copy the questions on the chalkboard for kids to consider.

1. What does the House of Usher look like outside? Inside?

2. Roderick Usher says he is suffering from "a morbid acuteness of the senses." What does he mean? What are the symptoms the narrator sees?

3. What happens to Madeline? Describe the place where she is buried.

4. Roderick's song "The Haunted Palace" starts off happy. What happens toward the end of the song? How does the song reflect what has happened to the House of Usher?

5. The narrator reads "The Mad Trist" to Roderick. How do the sounds and actions in "The Mad Trist" relate to what the narrator is hearing at that very moment in the house?

6. What alarms Roderick so much that he literally dies of shock? (At this point, you might share with your students teaching note 2 on page 12.)

7. As the narrator leaves in terror, what happens to the house? How have readers been prepared for the idea that the house might fall down? (Share with your students teaching note 3 on page 12.)

Follow-up Activities: Reading and Writing

1. Track the Story Ask reading or listening partners to work with other groups to review and discuss the story as they've outlined it on the page 16 reproducible. You might give each group another copy of the reproducible on which to enter their final ideas. Act as mentor by circulating among groups to offer help and suggestions as needed.

2. Class Discussion Allow about ten minutes for a general discussion of what students liked and didn't like about the story. Most "didn't likes" may focus on the difficulty of the vocabulary, or on the length of the story. Deal briefly with these negatives: explain that it is

the way people wrote in Poe's time. Then move on to the positives: it was scary; the descriptions really show the house, the sad state of Roderick, and the dilemma of the narrator; it was suspenseful, as readers wait to see what all those horrendous sounds in the basement will add up to!

3. Build an "Atmosphere" Vocabulary On the chalkboard, write the following story phrases, along with others you especially like. Ask students to tell what they feel, or see in their mind's eye, as they read or hear these phrases:

- vacant and eyelike windows
- dark draperies
- dark and intricate passages
- decayed trees and the gray wall
- sullen waters

If your students have copies of the story, or have jotted down words and phrases as they read or listened, invite them to share these atmosphere-setting devices with classmates. Add student contributions to your chalkboard list.

4. Write a Poe-like Story Distribute copies of the reproducible on page 17. Discuss how the web allows writers to plan an atmosphere and a setting for a tale of terror. Webs also provide space to note who the main characters are. Point out that the teller of the story is to be a first-person narrator, "I."

Students may wish to work independently or with a partner in this planning stage, and in the plotting of the story as well.

Remind students of Poe's standard for a good story—a unity of effect or impression. In this case, all the *word pictures* should focus on building an atmosphere of suspense, horror, and wonderment. As they conference and revise, partners should pay special attention to atmosphere and to the setting that contributes to it.

To publish stories, how about...

1. a read-aloud, with the lights turned down low?

2. a readers theater presentation? (See page 18 for hints.)

3. a class anthology, e.g., Our Tales of Terror? (The anthology can be developed as students continue their study of Poe.)

4. a synopsis of the student-story, to convince a filmmaker that the tale would make a great movie?

5. the student's tape-recorded reading of the story, for classmates to listen to?

Curriculum Connections

1. ART. If ever a story inspired vivid mental images, it must be this one! Encourage students to use Poe's descriptions of the Usher estate (the exterior of the house and its gloomy surroundings) to draw or paint a picture of what the narrator sees as he approaches the mansion, or what he sees as he flees, while the mansion collapses and disappears into the lake. Or suggest students use Poe's descriptions to draw an architectural floor plan of the mansion itself, noting such sites as the gloomy rooms in which Roderick mopes, the cellar in which Madeline is buried, and the location of the narrator's bedroom just above it. Ask students to label their architectural drawings with numbered captions that sequentially tell what happens in the various rooms.

2. MUSIC. Roderick Usher can tolerate only the sound of a guitar! If one of your students, or a community-resource person, plays guitar, then extend an invitation to improvise for the class a sing-along melody for Roderick's "The Haunted Palace." Discuss with students how guitar sounds make them feel. How are the sounds different from those played—say—on a drum, a piano, or a horn? Invite students to write lyrics for another guitar song that might appeal to Roderick's fragile sensibilities.

3. MEDIA. Since most kids nowadays are inundated with horror movies and gruesome TV dramas, you might as well use this exposure to point out relationships to Poe's works. If kids want to talk about the latest *Halloween* film, or whatever movie, ask them to focus their discussions on atmosphere and setting. What is the setting? How exactly does the film create a visual atmosphere of terror? How would Poe—with no movie director to do it for him— describe this setting and atmosphere in writing? Challenge students to write an "in Poe's words" synopsis of the movie or TV presentation.

4. TECHNOLOGY. Sounds pretty outlandish, that the Ushers' house could collapse all of a sudden! Yet newspapers nowadays often carry stories about bridges, roads, pipelines, and whole buildings that do just that. While the problem is mechanical—the untended, neglected infrastructure of cities— the potential stories could be very imaginative. Invite your superstar writers to create a newspaper story, set in modern times, that ends with the "Fall of (Something)"— (Brooklyn Bridge? Sears Tower? Space Needle?). Advise your writers to do some research about the structure before they begin to write, so that they can incorporate believable, factual details into their stories.

15

Name _____

Tracking the Story
"The Fall of the House of Usher"

A. What is the setting? _____
_____

B. What is the atmosphere? _____
_____

C. Who are the three main characters? Describe each one.

1. _____
_____
_____

2. _____
_____
_____

3. _____
_____
_____

D. Track the plot: In your opinion, what are the three most important events in the story?

1. _____
_____
_____

2. _____
_____
_____

3. _____
_____
_____

Name _____

Planning a Poe-like Story

Use what you're learning about Edgar Allan Poe's tales of terror to plan your very own tale of terror.

A. The Setting of My Story: _____
_____

B. The Atmosphere I'll Create in My Story: _____
_____
_____

Words and Phrases I Might Use to Create the Atmosphere:

Sounds: _____
Odors: _____
Sights: _____
Touch: _____

C. Main Characters for My Story

Me: I'll be the first-person narrator. Why am I in the setting I've described?
_____
_____

Two Other Main Characters (Name and describe each one.)

1. _____
_____
_____

2. _____
_____
_____

D. Plot Ideas: Write your plot ideas on the other side of this page.

Readers Theater
"The Masque of the Red Death"

Synopsis

The plot and problem are simple: In the outside world, a terrible contagious disease—"the Red Death," with its grisly symptoms and its unavoidable fatality—is killing off the population. Inside the bastion of his castle, Prince Prospero seeks to keep himself and a thousand of his noble friends safe from the disease by sealing the entrances and securing stores of food and other supplies that will last for months, until the disease outside has passed. Can Prospero succeed in this endeavor?

Prince Prospero decides to amuse his guests with a masqued ball. In elaborate and beautiful disguises, they whirl and dance through the party rooms of the castle. The *setting* is peculiar: each room is draped and decorated with a specific color; the seventh room, which Propsero tells his guests not to enter, is black, with red-paned windows. The *atmosphere*: eerie! It veers back and forth between noisy, enthusiastic "partying" and solemn stillness. Each time the huge clock sounds the hour, the orchestra stops playing and the guests stand still, as if they were frozen in time. Suddenly, an uninvited *character* appears at the party. He wears a costume that makes him look like a victim of the Red Death. Offended by this intruder (definitely a downer in his gruesome garb!), Prospero chases him into the seventh room, challenges him, then falls dead. The guests attack the intruder and discover that his "costume" is not a costume at all. He is indeed the Red Death itself, and the party-goers die immediately.

Teaching Notes

1. The real-life background: Poe saw many of his friends die during epidemics of cholera. This infectious disease, common all over the world many years ago, is caused by a microorganism found in polluted water which violently attacks the intestines. However, in Poe's day, people knew little or nothing about the cause of cholera, much less about a cure for it. Most victims died within 24 hours of contracting the disease. Nowadays, with cause and preventive methods known, modern medicine can often intervene to prevent cholera or to save its victims.

2. Did Poe intend a message in this story? Opinions vary. Maybe he meant to tell about how an epidemic can impact even the most secluded and protected elements of society. Or maybe he was warning rich and privileged people that they mustn't ignore the problems of ordinary people. Or maybe Poe was simply inspired by a horrendous situation—cholera—to write a great horror story. Or maybe he was doing all of these things!

Prereading/Acting Activities

Use Prior Knowledge
Invite students to discuss the following:
- Who gets invited to a party? Who may get left off the guest list? How might a person feel who is not invited to an important party? Remind students of the story "Sleeping Beauty." An uninvited guest appears anyway, and—enraged by her absence from the guest list—brings doom upon the princess and everyone in her house. Explain that "The Masque of the Red Death" includes an uninvited, unwelcomed guest.

- What diseases or addictions are people afraid of today? How do people try to protect themselves from these things? Explain that "The Masque of the Red Death" tells about a man who tries to ignore a disease that is raging around him. At this point, you may wish to share teaching note 1 on page 18 with your students.

Choose a Mode of Presentation
We're suggesting that students explore the story through readers theater. To prepare for this presentation, read the synopsis on page 18 to the class and summarize the teaching notes there.

Other presentation options: See page 6.

Focus on Literary Elements
Characters: Preview by prompting a discussion on main characters your students have read about or viewed who are "bad guys." Movies and TV shows should provide a lot of examples. What's interesting about these villains? What's terrifying about them? Ask students to read or listen for what's interesting and awful about Prince Prospero, the main character in "The Masque of the Red Death."

Theme: Explain to or review with students that a story's theme expresses a main idea that can be applied to everyday life. Provide some examples of themes, and invite students to identify stories they've read which develop them. Examples:
- Friendship is precious.
- You have to test yourself to discover your strengths.
- In the long run, you have to pay for your mistakes.

Ask students to think about the theme or themes of "The Masque of the Red Death" as they read it or act it out.

19

Preparing and Presenting the Play

1. Give a Copy of the Script to Each Student (pages 22–25). Explain that different groups of students will read the play aloud in front of the class, while classmates read along silently.

2. Preview With the class, review the cast of characters and scan the script to make sure students know how each speaker's lines are signaled and that the words in italics and parentheses suggest the tone of voice or gestures the speaker should use.

3. Discuss Optional Dramatic Devices The play can be presented with no props at all: the actors stand, or sit on stools, in front of the class as they read the script. However, some acting troupes may wish to embellish their performances with recorded music that fades in and out, with cymbals or a drum to replicate the chiming of the clock, or with lighting effects that indicate the colors of the different rooms. Point out that these options require one or two additional troupe members who can deliver the sounds or sights on cue.

4. Help Students Form Acting Troupes Familiarize yourself with the script so that you can act as mentor while groups assign roles. Make sure that all students who want a speaking role are assigned one. (Note that some characters speak elaborate dialogue, while other dialogue is comparatively simple.)

5. Provide Space and Time for Rehearsal Each acting group should have an opportunity to practice reading the script aloud together at least once before their presentation. A second run-through is always desirable. Groups that have opted for sounds and lighting may need additional preparation time.

6. Presentation Options

• On different days, each group presents its performance to the class. (Suggestion: Through your mentoring of the groups, determine which group has the play down solid. Have this group perform first. That way, actors in other groups will learn valuable performance tips.)

• Some groups may wish to perform the play by tape rather than in front of the class. Classmates or families at home can listen to and enjoy the taped performance.

• An acting group can perform the play for students in another classroom, in the school library, or for an audience of families.

• After all groups have performed, ask for an impromptu "switch roles" performance: Call on students at random to play a part other than their original one.

Curriculum Connections

1. ART/WRITING Ask students to imagine that they're presenting key scenes from "The Masque of the Red Death" to a movie producer, in hopes that the story will be adapted for a film. Each pictured scene should be accompanied by a caption that vividly describes what's happening. Display picture panels on a Movies-by-Poe bulletin board.

2. LITERARY ANALYSIS Distribute the reproducible on page 26. Preview the prompts. Students can carry them out independently or with a partner. After proofreading and writing a final copy, writers can put their letters in envelopes and place them in a letter grab bag: classmates choose a letter at random and read it aloud to the class or to a small group. After several letters have been read, invite your students to discuss the similarities and differences in their reactions to "The Masque of the Red Death."

3. MUSIC Students might bring to class tapes or CDs of music they feel capture the atmosphere of "The Masque of the Red Death." Modern or "old-fashioned," the music should reflect the wild, eerie, energetic whirling of the dancers in the story. As examples of your own to play for the class, consider using the following (all available in numerous recordings): Copland's "El Salon Mexico"; Liszt's "Tarantella"; Berlioz's "Sabbath," from his *Symphonie Fantastique*.

4. HEALTH/SCIENCE Up-to-date knowledge about the cause and conquest of infectious diseases can be reassuring as well as informative to students. After you present teaching note 1 on page 18, some students may want to get to the nitty-gritty. Invite them to research cholera to determine where and when it may occur nowadays, how people contract it, how it may be cured through modern medicine, and what steps disaster victims might take to avoid cholera altogether.

Encourage your researchers to extend their investigations: what other diseases—once considered fatal—are now often curable or treatable if caught in time? Examples are tuberculosis and malaria. What diseases have been almost wiped out by modern medicine? Examples are smallpox, diphtheria, leprosy, and polio.

After students present their findings to classmates, encourage a whole-class discussion on a different ending for "The Masque of the Red Death" if the story were set in modern times.

The Masque of the Red Death
Adapted from the story by Edgar Allan Poe

Characters
- Narrator
- Prince Prospero
- Prospero's Servant
- Citizens 1 and 2
- Noble 1
- Noble 2
- Noble 3
- The Uninvited Guest

SCENE ONE

Narrator: Outside Prince Prospero's castle, the Red Death rages! Victims fall ill in the morning and are dead by evening. Inside the barricaded castle, Prince Prospero seeks to protect himself and 1,000 of his rich and noble friends from the gruesome plague.

Citizen 1 *(from offstage)*: For pity's sake, let us in!

Servant *(to Prospero)*: My lord, the people outside beg for your protection!

Prospero: That is none of my affair! Let them die! Here in my home, my friends and I are safe. Are the doors and windows locked?

Servant: Yes, my lord.

Prospero: Have we enough food and water to last for several months?

Servant: Yes, my lord.

Prospero: Good! Then I and my friends shall entertain ourselves with parties until the plague has passed.

Citizen 2 *(from offstage)*: We need your help, Prince Prospero!

Prospero *(to Servant)*: Shoo that person away! *(Servant makes "shooing" gesture)* Good! Now let us prepare for a party, so that we can forget all this dying nonsense going on outside.

SCENE TWO

Narrator: Prince Prospero prepares his castle for a grand party. Each of the seven great rooms is decorated in a different color.

Noble 1 *(gesturing with enthusiasm)*: A room painted blue, with blue glass windows! And next, a room with purple windows and all the curtains and furniture in purple!

Noble 2 *(enthusiastically)*: A third room all in green! A fourth room all in orange! A fifth room all in white, and the sixth in violet! *(To Prospero:)* My lord, you have planned this party well!

Prospero: The colors will make us all happy as we party and dance through the rooms tonight.

Noble 3 *(gesturing offstage)*: But what about this seventh room? It's all in black, except for the windows, which are blood-red!

Prospero: Never mind that! We will never reach the seventh room. We will dance all night through the other six, one at a time.

Servant: My lord, shall I wind and set the great mahogany clock to strike the hours?

Prospero: Yes, do so, so that we can keep track of our merriment.

Citizen 1 *(from offstage)*: I plead with you again, Prospero, to let us in to the safety of your castle!

Citizen 2 *(from offstage)*: We are dying out here!

Prospero *(waving away the offstage voices)*: Away with you both! You dying people are not welcome here!

SCENE THREE

Narrator: What a party! A costume ball! The guests are dressed in outrageous disguises, richly decorated with jewels and rare cloth. Each guest wears an elaborate, beautiful mask. Nobody can tell who anybody really is. Around and around they whirl...

Noble 1 *(excited)*: We dance through the blue room and the purple room!

Noble 3 *(puzzled)*: Have you noticed? Each time the huge clock strikes the hour, we stop as if we were frozen. The music stops, as does all conversation! We're as silent and still as if we were dead!

Noble 2 *(happy)*: But then, when the clock stops striking, we dance again...through the green room, the orange room, the white room! This is a wonderful party!

Prospero: Are you having fun, my friends?

Nobles 1 and 2 *(in unison)*: Indeed we are, dear prince!

Noble 3 *(worried, to Prospero)*: Next we will dance into the violet room, my lord. And after the clock has chimed comes the seventh room, all draped in black and red. What awaits us there?

Prospero *(impatiently)*: Nothing at all! Why are you such a worrywart? Simply enjoy yourself within the safety of my castle!

Citizens 1 and 2 *(in unison from offstage)*: Let us in, Prospero!

Servant: People from the town are outside the gates, my lord!

Prospero *(angrily)*: Well, shoo them away, as usual!

SCENE FOUR

Narrator: An uninvited guest finds his way into Prospero's castle. What a gruesome sight he is! All the other guests are disguised in costumes of great beauty, but this intruder wears a mask that makes him look like a victim of the Red Death: All bloody! The eyes and mouth scarlet, and twisted in agony! Would you want a downer like that at your party? Prince Prospero certainly doesn't!

Servant: Beg pardon, my lord, but this person broke in!

Prospero *(angrily, to uninvited guest)*: How dare you intrude on my party? How dare you wear such an ugly costume?

Nobles 1 and 2 *(in unison, shuddering)*: Awful!

Uninvited Guest *(firmly and strongly)*: I always come uninvited! Nothing you do can keep me out. I can invade any party! And I am dressed as your worst nightmare. I laugh at your happy costumes, and at your rooms draped in cheery blue, purple, green, orange, white, and violet!

Prospero: I ask you to leave! Do you dare challenge my authority as ruler of this castle? If so, follow me into the seventh room, the room of black and red! There we will duel, and you will learn who is master here!

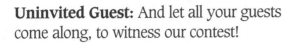

Uninvited Guest: And let all your guests come along, to witness our contest!

Noble 3 *(to Prospero)*: Don't go with him, my lord! *(To Nobles 1 and 2)* Don't follow! I feel that danger and doom await us!

Narrator: In spite of their friend's warning, Prince Prospero's guests rush after him to the black-and-red room. There they will witness a gruesome battle.

SCENE FIVE

Narrator: The battle begins!

Prospero *(as if using a sword against the guest)*: Take that, and that, ugly creature!

Guest *(laughing and unwounded)*: No mere sword can conquer me! And I need no sword to win a battle. I conquer simply through my presence. *(He points at Prospero, who keels over, dead.)* Prospero, your pride has brought your downfall.

Noble 1 *(bravely)*: Murderer! Take off your mask!

Noble 2: Only a coward will hide behind a false face!

Guest *(laughing)*: I warn you, there is nothing false about me!

Narrator: The Prince's noble friends attack the uninvited guest and try to rip off his disguise. But of course, it is not a disguise at all! The uninvited guest really is the Red Death.

Noble 3 *(gasping, dying)*: The uninvited guest has slain us all! Who will survive to tell this tale of pride and horror?

Citizen 1: Why, we will, of course. Some of us survived the Red Death. And then he moved on to other lands.

Citizen 2: We survivors took up our day-to-day lives again.

Narrator: But Prospero's castle will be silent forever.

Name _____

A Letter to Poe

Complete the letter by answering the questions in the margin.

Dear Mr. Poe,
I've explored your story "The Masque of the Red Death."
To me, the best quality of the story is _____
_____
_____
_____

Tell what you like best about the story.

To me, the most interesting character is _____ ,
because _____
_____
_____

Name your favorite character, and tell why.

I like the way you've developed the atmosphere of the story by
_____
_____
_____
_____

Pinpoint some ways Poe builds an atmosphere.

Here are a couple of suggestions for revising the story for
today's audiences: _____
_____
_____
_____

Summarize any ideas you have for revising the story.

        Sincerely,
        your fan,
        _____

Sign your name.

Group Work
"Ligeia," "Hop-Frog," and "The Tell Tale-Heart"

Synopses

"Ligeia": The narrator relates the virtues of his beloved first wife, Ligeia. She was darkly beautiful, intelligent, independent, and strong-minded—so strong-minded, in fact, that even as she died she protested that death would not conquer her, and predicted she would return to her husband. The widower, still grieving, then marries the fair-haired Lady Rowena, whom he does not like at all. Lady Rowena quickly sinks into a mysterious, fatal illness. But as she expires, the spirit and countenance of Ligeia takes over Rowena's body, and Ligeia rises from the sickbed to be reunited with her understandably horrified husband.

"Hop-Frog": Hop-Frog is a lamed fellow. He and his childhood friend, Tripetta, were kidnapped long ago to serve as jester and servant in the court of an evil king. The king terribly mistreats them both and finally insults Tripetta. When the king and his malign cohorts demand that Hop-Frog think up something "unusual" for their disguises at a masqued ball, Hop-Frog devises a gruesome pageant and a (very) gory revenge!

"The Tell-Tale Heart": The narrator is a madman who, like the more-sympathetic Roderick in "The Fall of the House of Usher," is particularly sensitive to sights and sounds. In this case, the narrator can't stand the sight of the clouded eye and the sound of the heartbeat of an old man whom he holds captive. He arranges the old man's death, and buries him. Yet the narrator fancies he can still hear the heartbeat of the dead man and supposes other people can also. He decides to confess his crime to the police investigators, who then visit to make inquires.

Teaching Notes

1. Do these stories relate to Poe's life? Maybe so! Like Ligeia, Poe's beloved wife died early. Like Hop-Frog, Poe felt mistreated (by his foster father and by literary critics). Like the narrator of "The Tell-Tale Heart," Poe may have felt that his own weaknesses and peculiarities would spell his downfall.

2. During Poe's lifetime, these three stories, like many others of Poe's tales of terror, were more appreciated in Europe than they were in America. The stories particularly impressed French writers of the time, who praised them and incorporated Poe's style and Gothic themes and atmospheres into their own work.

Prereading Activities

Use Prior Knowledge

Invite students to name stories, movies, TV programs, or songs that develop the following themes:

- Though you may lose someone or something you love, that beloved object may affect your life forever.

- A person who is mistreated or laughed at may seek revenge.

- Guilt for a misdeed or crime is a heavy burden.

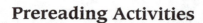

Explain that the Poe stories students will explore develop the themes above. Ask students to predict, on the basis of their explorations of "The Fall of the House of Usher" and "The Masque of the Red Death," the general atmospheres and settings Poe will use to develop these themes.

Choose a Mode of Presentation

Divide your students into three groups and assign a story to each group. Each group can do a detailed exploration of the story, using one of the two strategies that follow:

1. The Independent Reading Circle Strategy
Use this approach with students who can help one another move through complex narrative successfully by using the Reading Circle Cards on pages 30–32.

2. The Tell-and-Read Strategy
In Tell-and-Read, the teacher shares the story aloud 1) by telling summarized parts of it in his or her own way, 2) by reading verbatim excerpted portions of it to both move the story along and to familarize students with the author's style, and 3) by asking questions along the way to check comprehension.

What questions should you ask? Use the prompts on the reading circle cards; feel free to inject other questions of your own, and welcome and discuss additional questions that your students raise.

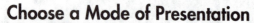's a way to present the opening sections of the story "Ligeia":

TELL: "Ligeia" is about the power of love and the power of life over death. The narrator has married an extraordinary woman named Ligeia. Here's how the narrator describes Ligeia:

READ: "In stature she was tall, somewhat slender, and, in her latter days, even emaciated. I would in vain attempt to portray the majesty, the quiet ease of her demeanor, or the incomprehensible lightness...of her footfall.... And her eyes!...large, shining!"

TELL: The narrator is also overwhelmed by Ligeia's intelligence and wisdom. He says...

READ: "I have spoken of the learning of Ligeia —such as I have never known in a woman. In the classical tongues was she deeply proficient....her knowledge was such as I have never known..."

USE THE QUESTIONS ON READING CIRCLE CARD 1, page 30, to prompt discussion. Continue in this manner through the story, choosing for READ passages the ones that you find most moving and important; and for TELLs, your own summaries of major events.

Follow-up Activities: Discussing and Writing

1. Discussing Literary Elements Bring your listeners and readers together to compare and contrast the elements of atmosphere, setting, characters, and theme in the three stories. Distribute copies of the reproducible on page 33 to facilitate the discussion. Also show a copy of the reproducible on an overhead projector, or copy part A on the chalkboard, to fill in as students share their ideas and reactions.

- Call on volunteers from the various groups to name the story they've studied and to briefly answer the following questions:

    What is the atmosphere of the story? (Examples: spooky, scary, gloomy, threatening.)

    What is the setting? (Examples: "Ligeia": gloomy mansions; "Hop-Frog": the court of an evil king; "The Tell-Tale Heart": an old house or dungeon.)

    Who are the main characters in the story you studied? Ask students to briefly describe these characters. (Examples: a woman who believes she can overcome death; a servant who hates his master; a crazy man who can't stand unusual sights and sounds.)

    What theme or themes do you find in the story? (See "Use Prior Knowledge" on page 28; encourage students to suggest additional themes in the story they've studied.)

- Ask students to work independently or with a partner to complete part A of the reproducible on page 33, based on their class discussion and the summaries you've jotted down on the overhead or chalkboard.

2. Writing an Overview of Poe's Tales of Terror Direct students' attention to part B of the page 33 reproducible. Ask them to use their notes from part A to write the paragraph. Students can work independently to draft, then work with a partner to revise and edit. To publish, ask students to read their paragraphs aloud to a small group of classmates. Key question: What do you learn by comparing and contrasting ideas about Poe and his work?

3. Revising Poe-like Stories, or Writing New Ones As a follow-up activity (page 14) after reading "The Fall of the House of Usher," students may have tried their hand at writing a tale of terror. Now students—with several other Poe stories under their belts and with additional insights into Poe's techniques—may wish to revise these stories. Or they may wish to write a second Poe-like story to incorporate their new insights. Student artists can draw illustrations for their classmates' stories, or start designing book covers for the class anthology they are planning.

Reading Circle Cards:
Ligeia

1. Why does the narrator admire Ligeia?

   What is your reaction to Ligeia?

2. What does Ligeia feel about the finality of death?

   What do you predict might happen after Ligeia dies?

3. Why does the narrator move to a new home?

   Describe the narrator's own bad habits or illness.

4. Describe Lady Rowena.

   How does the narrator feel about his new wife?

5. What does the narrator feel as Rowena dies?

   What happens as Rowena breathes her last breath?

6. Give your opinions:

   What is the theme of the story? Is the narrator imagining things, or is the last incident real? Explain.

Reading Circle Cards:
Hop-Frog

1. Describe Hop-Frog and Tripetta.

   How have they come to live in the king's court? What do they do there?

2. Describe the king and his followers.

   How does the king treat his servants?

3. What insulting action does the king take against Tripetta?

   What is Hop-Frog's reaction to this insult?

4. As the masked ball approaches, what does the king ask Hop-Frog to do?

   What do you suspect that Hop-Frog is planning?

5. Describe the costumes and procedures Hop-Frog devises for the king and his followers.

   What happens when the king follows Hop-Frog's plans?

6. How do you feel about what Hop-Frog has done in revenge?

   In your opinion, what is the theme of this story?

Reading Circle Cards:
The Tell-Tale Heart

1. Who narrates the story?

   According to the narrator, what is his mental state?

2. What is it about the old man that the narrator dislikes?

   Why would an unusual "eye" particularly upset a deranged person? What might the eye symbolize?

3. Why does the narrator kill the old man?

   What does he do next?

4. What eerie sensation does the narrator have after his victim is buried?

   Why do you think he has that sensation?

5. The narrator confesses to the crime even before he has been accused of it.
   Why does he do that?

6. Give your opinion:
   • What is the theme of the story?
   • Does this theme apply to real people today? Explain, or give some examples.

Name _____

A. Literary Elements in Poe's Stories

Typical ATMOSPHERES
_____
_____
_____
_____
_____
_____
_____
_____

Typical SETTINGS
_____
_____
_____
_____
_____
_____
_____
_____

Typical CHARACTERS
_____
_____
_____
_____
_____
_____
_____
_____

Typical THEMES
_____
_____
_____
_____
_____
_____
_____
_____

B. Writing an Overview

Imagine someone who has never read Poe's tales of terror! On a separate sheet of paper, write a paragraph that summarizes typical atmospheres, settings, characters, and themes a reader can expect to find in Poe's stories. Use vivid words and phrases that will make your audience eager to read these tales.

Readers Theater
"The Purloined Letter"

Synopsis

The villain (Minister D.) steals (purloins) an incriminating letter from the Queen of France and intends to blackmail her with it in order to further his own political ambitions. The queen begs the prefect (head) of the Paris police to get the letter back and return it to her. But, despite thorough searches of Minster D.'s home, the prefect can't find the letter. The prefect's friend, Dupin, guarantees to find and retrieve the letter. And so he does, finding the incriminating document "in plain sight," and further compounding the plot by leaving a fake document "in plain sight" of Minister D., so that it will be a long time before the villain discovers that his evil intent has been foiled.

Teaching Notes

1. "The Purloined Letter" is one of three stories Poe wrote about the detective C. Auguste Dupin. (The other two are "The Mystery of Marie Roget" and "The Murders in the Rue Morgue.") These stories represent the very beginning of the detective-story genre. The paradigm Poe established—a highly intellectual main character who uses logic to intercept a criminal—was the model used by Conan Doyle in his Sherlock Holmes stories and by almost all major detective-story writers today. Indeed, the annual prize for a great detective story is called "The Edgar," in honor of the man who invented this kind of tale.

2. What a contrast the logical, cerebral, sensible Dupin is with the main characters students have encountered in Poe's tales of terror, who are driven by emotion and even insanity! You can use this contrast between the detective story and the horror story to point out the following:

• A main character's personality often shapes the plot. For example, the mental and physical illnesses of Roderick Usher and his sister lead to doom and downfall. The common sense and logic of detective Dupin lead to a "happy ending" (happy for the queen, at least!).

• A writer may try his or her hand at a variety of genres. In addition to terror tales and detective stories, Poe wrote poetry (coming up!) and literary criticism (a.k.a. "the book review"), and originated the science-fiction story.

- On page 44 of the play script, the prefect and Dupin exchange lines that sarcastically comment on how poets were viewed by the general public. You may find a point in the class discussion of the play in which to call attention to these lines. What do they indicate about Poe's awareness of how people judged him and his work?

Prereading-Acting Activities

Use Prior Knowledge
Invite students to discuss the following:
- Who are some fictional detectives and criminals you've read about, or viewed on TV and in the movies? In what particularly intriguing mysteries or problems were they involved?
- Compare the stories you've discussed. Which ones stress the physical powers or strengths of detectives and villains? Which ones stress their intelligence and skill?
- Share teaching note 1 on page 34 with students. Then ask them to predict what the characters and plot will be like in "The Purloined Letter."

Focus on Literary Elements
Plot: Distribute the reproducible on page 48 (The Elements of a Plot). Preview plot components and their definitions. Explain that as students read, perform, or listen to "The Purloined Letter" they should note how the components are covered. Students will use their notes during the writing activity described on page 36.

Preparing and Presenting the Play
1. Give a Copy of the Script to Each Student (pages 40–47). Then review/introduce/adapt the Preparing and Presenting ideas.

2. Provide Some Background After previewing the script for "The Purloined Letter" on your own, you may wish to introduce some thoughts for actors to consider as they interpret the characters.
- Why is the queen so anxious to hide the letter from her husband, the king? That is, what might the letter reveal? The first possibility, of course, is that it is a love letter. Another possibility is that the letter may reveal a political plot the queen is preparing against the king.
- The play presents a battle of wits between two of the characters; the other characters simply provide a background for this battle. Who are these two "cleverest" characters? (Dupin; Minister D.) How are they alike? Different?

3. Encourage Students to Build on Previous Dramatic Experience If your students have performed "The Masque of the Red Death," encourage them to discuss what they've learned about presenting plays, and how they'll use what they've learned in presenting "The Purloined Letter." Focus on the "must's":
- A Well-Prepared Acting Troupe—props, read-throughs, rehearsals, considerations of options such as sound effects.

• A Savvy, Alert Audience—What will the audience expect from the actors? Examples: clear diction and speech that's loud enough to be heard in the back row; distinct voices for the different characters, with plenty of "expression"; a pace that's just right: actors shouldn't read too fast. You might ask students to construct an Audience Checklist that incorporates the considerations above. The list will not only serve as a good guide for a follow-up discussion of each presentation, but also as a guide for the next troupe on the schedule.

Curriculum Connections

1. CAREER SKILLS: On the chalkboard, list the following skills. Invite students to discuss how Dupin—in his career as a detective—uses these skills to bring the case of the purloined letter to a successful conclusion. (Note: During the discussion, which bears on plot, students can use and amend their notes on their copies of the page 48 reproducible.)

- Determining the problem
- Understanding motives
- Planning an approach
- Using keen observation skills
- Taking calculated risks
- Solving the problem in an original way

Invite students to discuss how the same skills are useful in almost any career. How are they used, for example, by a computer whiz? A doctor? A scientist aboard a space shuttle? A writer? An artist? A teacher?

2. CRITICAL VIEWING: Show a videotape of one of the Sherlock Holmes mysteries. Preface the showing by asking students to watch for ways Holmes uses the skills listed in 1, above, to solve the mystery. Follow up by having students discuss their observations.

3. TECHNOLOGY/SCIENCE: Dupin and Holmes work by their wits alone, using the skills listed in 1, above. Nowadays, of course, science and technology provide additional ways to track and identify suspects. Examples are DNA testing, fingerprints, wiretaps, video-surveillance cameras, voiceprints, and hot lines telling citizens how they can call in possible clues to a perpetrator's identity and whereabouts. Ask interested students to discuss and report on these methods and/or to list them for possible use in the writing activity that follows.

4. WRITING: In a quick go-around, ask students to share the notes they've made about plot on the page 48 reproducible. Then distribute the reproducible on page 49, Planning a Mystery Story. Preview what students are asked to do. Encourage them to use ideas from other mysteries they've read. (Note: A great book for students to use as they plan mystery stories is *The Usborne Detective's Handbook* [Usborne Publishing Ltd, 1991]. This amusingly illustrated paperback for kids shows almost every detail a mystery-story writer might wish to cover.)

- Some students may enjoy revamping the play script of "The Purloined Letter" to set it in modern times, using the technology and science ideas they've garnered from activity 3.
- Have students work with writing partners to discuss, revise, and edit their mystery stories. Again, students can use the plot steps on page 48 as writing and conferencing guidelines.

5. CIVICS/HISTORY: To bring home to students the reality of political shenanigans like the one in "The Purloined Letter," you may wish to assign student teams to research and report on real-life political dilemmas, such as the Teapot Dome "scandal"; the duel between Aaron Burr and Alexander Hamilton; the Benedict Arnold case; Napoleon's exile to Elba; the ouster of the Shah of Iran. Encourage student teams to present their findings in the form of readers theater, playing the parts of characters who present their different views of the situation.

6. VISUAL SKILLS: Minister D., in "The Purloined Letter," placed the evidence "in plain sight." As a challenge to students' visual acuity, invite them—one at a time over a period of days, and in private—to place a document or other article "in plain sight," give a mysterious clue to classmates (e.g., "an astounding color"; "something good to eat"; "a message that will free you of today's homework"), and then challenge classmates to find the article.

Bringing the Stories Together

Use the following activities to bring together main concepts about all of the Poe stories your students have studied.

1. ART: Invite students to form groups to plan and construct big wall maps that show their own renditions of the places where the Poe stories they've read take place. Encourage a lot of original input and imagination for rendering the places in map format: the house of the Ushers, the castle of Prince Prospero, the two gloomy homes of the narrator in "Ligeia," the castle where Hop-Frog carries out his gruesome revenge, the house where the deranged narrator in "The Tell-Tale Heart" buries his hapless victim, and the home of the wicked thief in "The Purloined Letter."

Suggest that groups provide clues through captions or dialogue balloons that will help their classmates identify the story and main characters (see example on next page). After each map has been featured and discussed, display them all under the banner POE LAND. Students might use the display for reference as they play a Poe trivia game (see number 2).

2. GAMES: **Trivial Poe-Suit.** Appoint a couple of emcees to pose questions about Poe's stories to classroom Trivia Teams. Explain that emcees' clues and questions should be clear as well as fun. Examples:

> She screamed! She hollered! She was an underground lady!
> (Answer: Madeline, in "The Fall of the House of Usher")

Which Poe character wore a disguise that was not a disguise? (the last guest in "The Masque of the Red Death")

Name three Poe characters who seem to live even after they're dead. (Ligeia; the old man in "The Tell-Tale Heart"; Madeline Usher)

Poe-Nopoly. Suggest that groups make a board game based on places and characters in Poe's stories. Squares on the game might indicate moves like the following:

> Buy the House of Usher.
> Bonus Point: Move a square ahead for finding the purloined letter.
> You lose! Caught in Prince Prospero's seventh room! Move back six squares.
> You're Hop-Frog! Hop two squares ahead.

Poe Pantomime. Invite students who like acting to pantomime three main events in the life of a character in a Poe story. Caution students that this is not as easy as it sounds, since many Poe characters express the same feelings of despair and puzzlement. Your actors will have to make their characters very clear wordlessly, using only gestures and movements. Specify a time limit (e.g., 20 seconds); if needed, provide time for private rehearsal. After the audience guesses the character, discuss the clues they used.

3. AN ANTHOLOGY: If your students have carried out several of the activities in the foregoing pages, suggest that they bring the results together in an anthology to share with families and with students in other classrooms.

- Explain or review that an *anthology* is a collection of materials on a broad topic, organized under subheads. For example, the work your students have done so far falls into the broad topic Our Responses to the Work of Edgar Allan Poe.
- Review and list on the chalkboard, with students, the subheads that might identify the ways they've responded to Poe's work, e.g., through discussion, pictures, dramas, tapes, musical interpretations, games, and original stories.
- Ask the class to appoint a committee of four or five members to collect classmates' work and organize it according to the subheads the class as a whole has determined. The committee drafts a table of contents and presents it to the class for comment and amendment. (NOTE: Make sure that each and every student's contribution is included in the anthology.)
- After considering and incorporating classmates' input, the committee compiles the anthology into an organized "package" to present as a resource for the classroom, as a project summary for the school as a whole, or as a presentation for visiting members of families at home.

An Example of an Anthology

Poe and Us

Our Gruesome Stories Inspired by Poe
The Cat and the Bat .... Lucie Medwark
Ligeia's Tell-Tale Heart .... Jaime Esposito
Hop-Frog and the Purple Death .... Awanda Shane

Stories on Tape
"The Fall of the House of Usher" .... As Read Aloud by Tim Reis and Kim Soo
"The Purloined Letter" .... As performed by Acting Troupe 1

Art Inspired by Poe's Stories
A Fold-Out Map: Settings of Poe Stories .... Jean Chin
Costumes for Poe Characters .... Lee Gerber

Poe Sounds On Tape
Rodney Usher's Song. .... Kevin McCloud
Sound Effects for
"The Masque of the Red Death" .... Consuela Uribe and Ross Hewit

The Purloined Letter
Edgar Allan Poe (Adapted by Tom Conklin)

Characters
- Dupin, a private detective in Paris
- Edgar, Dupin's best friend
- Prefect of Police, the head of the Paris police force
- King, the ruler of France
- Queen, the King's young wife
- Minister D., a scoundrel who works for the King
- Narrator (The Narrator is Edgar, looking back on what happened.)

SCENE ONE

Narrator: Just after dark one gusty autumn evening, I was enjoying a visit with my friend, C. August Dupin. As we sat in silence, the door was thrown open and in came our old acquaintance, the Prefect of Police.

Dupin *(standing)*: Greetings, my friend! Have a seat while I light the lamps. To what do we owe the honor of this visit?

Prefect: I have come to ask your opinion on something, Dupin. It's official business that is causing me a great deal of trouble.

Dupin *(sitting)*: Ah! If it is anything requiring thought, we should discuss it while sitting in the dark.

Prefect *(chuckling)*: Now, there's another one of your odd notions!

Narrator: The Prefect called everything "odd" that was beyond his own comprehension. He lived in a world full of "oddities."

Edgar: What is the difficulty now? A murder?

Prefect: Oh, no, nothing like that. The fact is, the mystery is very simple indeed. I don't doubt that we can solve it ourselves. But then I thought Dupin would like to hear the details of the case, because it is so...well...odd.

Dupin: A mystery that is simple and odd.

Prefect: Why, yes. And not exactly that, either. The fact is, we have been puzzled because the mystery is so simple, yet it has us baffled.

Dupin: Perhaps it is the simplicity of the case which baffles you.

Prefect *(laughing)*: What nonsense!

Dupin: Perhaps the mystery is a little too plain...

Prefect *(laughing harder)*: Oh, good heavens! Who ever heard of such an idea?

Dupin: ...A little too self-evident.

Prefect *(laughing hysterically)*: Ha! Ha! Ha! Oh, Dupin, you will be the death of me yet!

Edgar: And what are the facts of this mystery?

Prefect: I will tell you. But before I begin, let me caution you that this case demands the greatest secrecy. I would lose my job if anyone found out I told you about the case.

Edgar: Proceed.

Dupin: Or not.

Prefect: Well then, here are the facts....

SCENE TWO

Narrator: The prefect told us his story. It started a few months before, when the Queen of France received a letter. She was reading it, alone in the royal rooms, when the king entered.

King: My dear, what is that you are reading?

Queen *(startled)*: This? Oh, it is nothing! *(to herself)* He must not read this letter! It contains my personal secrets—things that the king must never know!

Narrator: The queen began to hide the letter in a drawer, then decided it best to simply toss it onto her desk, so as not to arouse suspicion. At that instant, Minister D. entered the room.

Minister D. *(bowing)*: Your majesties, thank you for seeing me. I have a few matters of business to discuss.

King: You may proceed.

Minister D.: Thank you. But her majesty the Queen seems nervous.

Queen *(eyeing the letter)*: Oh, it is nothing.

Minister D. *(following her glance)*: I see.

Narrator: Minister D., being a bold scoundrel, immediately saw that the letter was important to the queen. What is more, he could see that she wished to hide it from the king. Minister D. placed a letter he had brought with him onto the desk next to the queen's letter, then began discussing business. After 15 minutes or so, he deliberately picked up the queen's letter, leaving his own.

Queen *(gasping)*: No!

Minister D.: Is something wrong, your highness?

King: What is it, dear?

Queen: Oh...er...nothing.

Minister D. *(smiling with malice)*: Very good. I will leave you now. *(bowing to the king)* Good day, your majesty. *(bowing to the queen)* Your highness, I'm sure we will talk soon.

SCENE THREE

Edgar: So it's blackmail!

Prefect: Exactly. Minister D. has the letter. He threatens to give it to the king, unless the queen does just as he asks. Minister D. has used his power to gain political advantage. The queen is desperate to get the letter back, and has given the job to me.

Dupin: And no better detective could be desired— or even imagined.

Prefect: You flatter me—but it is possible that was her majesty's opinion, too.

Edgar: Is it certain that Minister D. still has the letter?

Prefect: He must. For his blackmail to work, he must be in a position to show the king the letter immediately. If he had already done so, I am sure that all of Paris would know!

Edgar: But you are quite skilled in these investigations. You have done this sort of thing many times before.

Prefect: Oh, yes. And for this reason I had great hopes. Minister D. is seldom home at night. I have keys, as you know, which can open any room or cabinet in Paris. For the past three months we have been busy ransacking Minister D.'s apartment. To no avail—we have not found the letter.

Edgar: Is it possible that Minister D. is carrying the letter with him?

Prefect: No. Three times I have had patrolmen waylay Minister D. and search him. He did not have the letter with him.

Dupin: You could have spared yourself the trouble. Minister D. is not altogether a fool, and would have expected these searches.

Prefect: Perhaps he is not a fool, but then he is a poet, which is almost the same thing.

Dupin *(smiling)***:** True...although I have been guilty of writing verse myself.

Edgar: Did you thoroughly search Minister D.'s apartment?

Prefect: Of course! We took our time and searched everywhere. We opened every possible drawer...

Edgar: How about "secret" drawers?

Prefect: There is no such thing to the trained eye. We probed the furniture cushions with long needles. We carefully took apart the tables and chairs—

Edgar: Why on earth did you do that?

Prefect: A letter could be hidden in a hollow leg or under the top of a table or seat of a chair.

Dupin: Was the letter hidden in this fashion?

Prefect: No. We put the furniture back together. Then we looked behind mirrors and pictures, in the mattress and bedclothes, behind curtains and under carpets. Then we searched the building itself. We divided its surface into sections, which we numbered. We examined every square inch with a microscope, searching for a secret compartment. Then we searched the houses on either side of Minister D.'s house.

Edgar: The two other houses! You have had a great deal of trouble!

Prefect *(blushing)***:** Yes. But her majesty has offered a substantial reward.

Edgar: Reward or no, you have not found the letter. You must be mistaken in thinking Minister D. has it in his rooms.

Prefect: I am afraid you are right. Dupin, what do you think I should do?

Dupin: Keep looking.

Prefect: Is that the best advice you can give?

Dupin *(shrugging his shoulders)*: As you said, the letter must be somewhere close at hand. You simply haven't found it yet. Do you have a description of the letter?

Prefect *(sighing)*: Yes, I do.

Narrator: The prefect took out a notebook and proceeded to read a detailed description of the missing document. After he finished reading the description, he left, more depressed than I had ever seen him before.

SCENE FOUR

Narrator: About a month later the prefect paid us another visit.

Edgar: Well, Prefect, what about the purloined letter? Did you find it?

Prefect: No, confound it, although I followed Dupin's advice and re-searched Minister D.'s rooms. It was wasted time, as I knew it would be.

Dupin: How much was the reward offered, did you say?

Prefect: Why, quite a lot. I—er—I hesitate to say exactly how much. But it's big enough that I would gladly write a check in the amount of 50,000 francs to anyone who could give me the letter.

Dupin: In that case, get out your checkbook. When you have signed a check to me for that amount, I will give you the letter.

Narrator: I was astounded. The prefect was absolutely thunderstruck. He stared silently at my friend, then took out his checkbook, wrote a check for 50,000 francs, and handed it to Dupin. My friend studied it carefully for a moment, slipped it into his pocket, then unlocked his desk drawer. He took out a letter and handed it to the prefect.

Prefect *(his eyes popping out)*: But—but—how?!

Narrator: Then, without another word, the prefect rushed out of our rooms with the letter.

Dupin: The police are very able...in their way. Unfortunately, they are no brighter or stupider than the mass of people. Their investigations often fail when they encounter a criminal smarter than they are—and often when they deal with criminals who are not as smart.

Edgar: But they conducted a thorough search!

Dupin: Of course. But they searched in places where they themselves might have hidden the letter! They did not think that Minister D., who is no fool, would anticipate that his rooms would be searched. Of course, he would never hide the letter behind a mirror, or in a hollow table leg, because if he did, it would certainly be found. He would choose a simpler place to hide it. In fact—he would choose not to hide it at all!

Edgar: I think I understand your reasoning. But how did you manage to get hold of the letter?

Dupin: It was simple. I took it!

SCENE FIVE

Narrator: Dupin told me how he paid a visit to Minister D. himself.

Minister D. *(yawning)*: Why, hello, Dupin. What brings you to my rooms?

Dupin: I was in the neighborhood and thought I would stop in for a chat.

Minister D.: Come in, my friend. It is good to see you. But why are you wearing dark glasses?

Dupin: My eyes are tired and the light bothers them.

Narrator: Dupin really wore the glasses so that his eyes could search the room without Minister D. suspecting. It did not take long for Dupin to find what he was looking for. His eyes soon fell on a cheap card rack which dangled from a dirty blue ribbon beneath the fireplace mantel. In the rack, plain to see, was a letter. Unlike the purloined letter, it was dirty and crumpled, with a woman's handwriting on the outside.

Dupin: Thank you for seeing me, sir. I have enjoyed our chat.

Minister D.: So have I. Please feel free to call again.

Narrator: Dupin left the room.

Minister D.: Dupin! Wait! *(Dupin is gone)* The fool. He left his snuffbox behind!

SCENE SIX

Narrator: The next day, Dupin returned to the rooms of Minister D.

Dupin: I'm sorry to trouble you, my friend. I forgot something yesterday.

Minister D.: Your snuffbox. Here it is—what is that?!

Narrator: A sound like gunfire cracked through the air, followed by screams. Minister D. rushed to the window. As Minister D. looked out the window, Dupin walked over to the mantle, took the ragged letter from the rack, and replaced it with an exact duplicate he had made.

Minister D. *(turning from the window)*: It is nothing. Some prankster burst a balloon. Well, Dupin, will you stay to chat?

Dupin: I am afraid not, my friend. I have what I came for!

SCENE SEVEN

Narrator: Dupin smiled with satisfaction as he told me his story.

Dupin: Of course, the "prankster" with the balloon was an agent I had hired to distract Minister D.

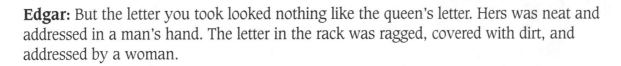

Edgar: But the letter you took looked nothing like the queen's letter. Hers was neat and addressed in a man's hand. The letter in the rack was ragged, covered with dirt, and addressed by a woman.

Dupin: Of course. It was so unlike the queen's letter—in every detail—that I knew it must be a fake. When I got back here, I found the queen's letter wrapped up inside the false letter.

Edgar: Does Minister D. know he has been had?

Dupin: I doubt it. The copy I made of his letter is perfect. He has no reason to open it up—not until the queen defies him. When that happens, he is in for a rude surprise.

Edgar: Oh, yes? What did you say in the letter you left?

Dupin: Oh, just a personal message. Something along the lines that scoundrels can hide in plain sight—but not forever!

Name _____

The Elements of a Plot

PLOT *is the series of events that make up a story. Write notes to tell about the plot of* "The Purloined Letter."

Plot Elements **My Notes**

INTRODUCTION: Who are the main characters in the story?

CONFLICT: What is the conflict, or problem that has to be solved?

COMPLICATIONS: What stands in the way of solving the conflict?

CLIMAX: What daring or exciting action takes place that helps to solve the problem?

RESOLUTION: How do the main characters feel, now that the problem is solved? (Include the villain's feelings in your analysis.)

Name _____

Planning a Mystery Story

Use the Plot Steps below to plan your own mystery story. Refer to "Elements of a Plot" for definitions. Suggestion: Many writers begin by thinking about and noting the conflict their story will deal with.

- Climax
- Conflict
- Complications
- Resolution
- Introduction

Four Poems by Edgar Allan Poe to Read Together

General Suggestions

1. We suggest you read and study the poems in the order presented here.

2. Before you read the first poem, distribute the reproducibles on pages 77–80, "Poe's Wonderful Words." Explain that this glossary defines many of the difficult or unfamiliar words in each poem in the order of the words' appearances. Students can preview the list before reading the poem, and/or refer to it later when preparing the poem for group presentation. Encourage partners to try the "Challenges" in the glossary and to share their results with classmates.

3. Distribute the reproducibles of the poem. Then, as chief reader for your class, read the poem aloud in its entirety as students follow along silently with their copies. Or you may prefer to have students follow along as they listen to a tape recording of the poem.

4. The teaching notes for each poem suggest what to stress as you read aloud, how students can proceed in their own read-alouds, and how they can follow up by applying elements of Poe's poetry to their own writing.

The Raven

Synopsis

In this, the most famous of Poe's poems, the speaker—a reclusive fellow just recovering from the death of Lenore, the lady he loved—recounts how a raven suddenly appeared and perched in his study. The raven knows one word—"nevermore." The poem's impact derives not only from its rhymes and rhythms, but also from the way it moves in mood from simple curiosity (What is this peculiar bird doing here?) into a feeling of inescapable gloom through the significance of the word "nevermore" as the raven croaks it in response to the speaker's questions. At first, "nevermore" seems simply to be the raven's name; then the word becomes an answer to when the raven intends to leave the speaker's house; eventually, "nevermore" is the answer to the speaker's query about when he will escape his suffering over the loss of Lenore.

Teaching Notes

1. As you read aloud, emphasize rhythm by "leaning on" the accented words or syllables. Example:

> Once **up**on a midnight **dreary**, while I **pondered**, weak and **weary**,
> Over **many** a quaint and **curious** volume of **forgotten lore** —
> While I **nodded** nearly **napping**, sudden**ly** there came a **tapping**,
> As of **some**one gently **rapping**, rapping at my **chamber door**

You might ask students to underline on their copies the stressed words or syllables as you read the stanzas again. Follow up by discussing with students how the steady rhythm gives the poem a songlike, musical quality. Invite volunteers to recite parts of modern lyrics, for example, in rap songs they know, that create rhythm through the performers' regular stress on words or syllables.

2. Briefly review rhyme. Through their previous experiences with poetry, most of your students will be able to identify the end rhymes in "The Raven." Examples: in the first stanza, *lore, door, more*; in the second stanza, *Lenore, floor, evermore*.

Challenge students to look for internal rhyme: the use of rhyming words within a line. Examples: Stanza I: *dreary, weary; napping, tapping*; Stanza II: *remember, December; morrow, borrow*; Stanza III: *uncertain, curtain; thrilled, filled; beating, repeating*.

3. Discuss the poem's content. Focus on feelings. What are the speaker's feelings in the first couple of verses? How and why do his feelings change? Ask students to give their reactions to the speaker: Is he only imagining that the raven knows about his grief? Is the speaker's grief a natural or an unusual reaction to the loss of a loved one?

4. Invite students to read aloud. Explain how the marginal numerals on the reproducible suggest how four readers can present the poem.

Have students organize foursomes and assign parts. Provide practice time, and act as mentor as groups practice. Are kids capturing the rhythm of the poem? Are they using the dramatic voices they practiced in presenting the plays "The Masque of the Read Death" and "The Purloined Letter"? Over a period of days, invite each group to present its rendition of the poem for readers theater or via tape recordings.

Follow-up

- To help students identify Poe's "sound" techniques, invite them to use the reproducible on page 59.
- Students can use the reproducible on page 60 to plan a poem of their own, using what they have learned through their read-alouds and discussion of "The Raven."

The Raven
A Poem by Edgar Allan Poe

Speaker	
1	

I

2	Once upon a midnight dreary, while I pondered, weak and weary.
	Over many a quaint and curious volume of forgotten lore —
3	While I nodded, nearly napping, suddenly there came a tapping,
	As of someone gently rapping, rapping at my chamber door —
4	" 'Tis some visitor," I muttered, "tapping at my chamber door —
1	Only this and nothing more."

II

2	Ah, distinctly I remember it was in the bleak December;
	And each separate dying ember wrought its ghost upon the floor.
3	Eagerly I wished the morrow; — vainly I had sought to borrow
	From my books surcease of sorrow — sorrow for the lost Lenore —
4	For the rare and radiant maiden whom the angels name Lenore —
1	Nameless *here* for evermore.

III

2   And the silken, sad, uncertain rustling of each purple curtain
Thrilled me — filled me with fantastic terrors never felt before;
3   So that now, to still the beating of my heart, I stood repeating
" 'Tis some visitor entreating entrance at my chamber door; —
4   Some late visitor entreating entrance at my chamber door; —
1   This it is and nothing more."

IV

2   Presently my soul grew stronger; hesitating then no longer,
3   "Sir," said I, "or Madam, truly your forgiveness I implore;
4   But the fact is I was napping, and so gently you came rapping,
And so faintly you came tapping, tapping at my chamber door,
That I scarce was sure I heard you" — here I opened wide the door; —
1   Darkness there and nothing more.

V

2   Deep into that darkness peering, long I stood there wondering, fearing.
Doubting, dreaming dreams no mortal ever dared to dream before;
3   But the silence was unbroken, and the stillness gave no token,
And the only word there spoken was the whispered word, "Lenore?"
4   This I whispered, and an echo murmured back the word, "Lenore!"
1   Merely this and nothing more.

VI

2	Back into the chamber turning, all my soul within me burning,
	Soon again I heard a tapping somewhat louder than before.
3	"Surely," said I, "surely that is something at my window lattice;
4	Let me see, then, what thereat is, and this mystery explore —
	Let my heart be still a moment and this mystery explore; —
1	'Tis the wind and nothing more!"

VII

2	Open here I flung the shutter, when, with many a flirt and flutter,
	In there stepped a stately Raven of the saintly days of yore;
3	Not the least obeisance made he; not a minute stopped or stayed he;
	But, with mien of lord or lady, perched above my chamber door —
4	Perched upon a bust of Pallas just above my chamber door —
1	Perched, and sat, and nothing more.

VIII

2   Then this ebony bird beguiling my sad fancy into smiling,
By the grave and stern decorum of the countenance it wore,
"Thought thy crest be shorn and shaven, thou," I said, "art sure no craven,
Ghastly grim and ancient Raven wandering from the Nightly shore —
Tell me what thy lordly name is on the Night's Plutonian shore!"
1   Quoth the Raven "Nevermore."

IX

3   Much I marvelled this ungainly fowl to hear discourse so plainly.
Though its answer little meaning — little relevancy bore;
For we cannot help agreeing that no living human being
Ever yet was blessed with seeing bird above his chamber door —
Bird or beast upon the sculptured bust above his chamber door,
1   With such name as "Nevermore."

X

4   But the Raven, sitting lonely on the placid bust, spoke only
That one word, as if his soul in that one word he did outpour.
Nothing further then he uttered - not a feather then he fluttered —
Till I scarcely more than muttered "Other friends have flown before —
On the morrow *he* will leave me, as my Hopes have flown before."
1   Then the bird said "Nevermore."

XI

2	Startled at the stillness broken by reply so aptly spoken,
	"Doubtless," said I, "what it utters is its only stock and store
	Caught from some unhappy master whom unmerciful Disaster
	Followed fast and followed faster till his songs one burden bore —
1	Till the dirges of his Hope that melancholy burden bore
	Of 'Never – nevermore.'"

XII

3	But the Raven still beguiling my sad fancy into smiling,
	Straight I wheeled a cushioned seat in front of bird, and bust and door;
4	Then, upon the velvet sinking, I betook myself to linking
	Fancy unto fancy, thinking what this ominous bird of yore —
1	What this grim, ungainly, ghastly, gaunt, and ominous bird of yore
	Meant in croaking "Nevermore."

XIII

2   This I sat engaged in guessing, but no syllable expressing
To the fowl whose fiery eyes now burned into my bosom's core;

3   This and more I sat divining, with my head at ease reclining
On the cushion's velvet lining that the lamp-light gloated o'er,

1   But whose velvet-violet lining with the lamp-light gloating o'er
        She shall press, ah, nevermore!

XIV

4   Then, methought, the air grew denser, perfumed from an unseen censer
Swung by seraphim whose foot-falls tinkled on the tufted floor.

2   "Wretch," I cried, "thy God hath lent thee — by these angels he hath sent thee
Respite — respite and nepanthe from thy memories of Lenore;
Quaff, oh quaff this kind nepenthe and forget this lost Lenore!"

1   Quoth the Raven "Nevermore."

XV

3   "Prophet!" said I, "thing of evil! — prophet still, if bird or devil! —
Whether Tempter sent, or whether tempest tossed thee here ashore,
Desolate yet all undaunted, on this desert land enchanted —
On this home by Horror haunted — tell me truly, I implore —

4   Is there — *is* there balm in Gilead? — tell me — tell me, I implore!"

1   Quoth the Raven "Nevermore."

XVI

2   "Prophet!" said I, "thing of evil! — prophet still if bird or devil!
By that Heaven that bends above us — by that God we both adore —
Tell this soul with sorrow laden if, within the distant Aidenn,
It shall clasp a sainted maiden whom the angels name Lenore —
Clasp a rare and radiant maiden whom the angels name Lenore."
1   Quoth the Raven "Nevermore."

XVII

3   "Be that word our sign of parting, bird or fiend!" I shrieked, upstarting —
"Get thee back into the tempest and the Night's Plutonian shore!
4   Leave no black plume as a token of that lie thy soul hath spoken!
Leave my loneliness unbroken! — quit the bust above my door!
2   Take thy beak from out my heart, and take thy form from off my door!"
1   Quoth the Raven "Nevermore."

XVIII

2   And the Raven, never flitting, still is sitting, *still* is sitting
On the pallid bust of Pallas just above my chamber door;
3   And his eyes have all the seeming of a demon's that is dreaming,
And the lamp-light o'er him streaming throws his shadow on the floor;
4   And my soul from out that shadow that lies floating on the floor
1   Shall be lifted — nevermore!

Name _____

Exploring Poe Sounds

Study the definitions and the examples in the first column. In the second column, list other examples you find in "The Raven."

1. RHYME: A word having the same last sound as another

A. *END RHYME*: words that rhyme at the END of a line of poetry

EXAMPLES:
Stanza I: *lore, door, more*
Stanza II: *Lenore, floor, evermore*

Other examples of
END RHYME in "The Raven"
_____
_____
_____
_____
_____
_____
_____

B. *INTERNAL RHYME*: words that rhyme WITHIN a line of poetry

EXAMPLES:
Stanza II: *remember, December*
Stanza III: *thrilled, filled*

Other examples of *INTERNAL RHYME* in "The Raven"
_____
_____
_____
_____
_____
_____
_____

2. ALLITERATION: a repetition of the same first sound in words that are close together in a line of poetry

EXAMPLES:
Stanza I: nearly napping
Stanza II: rare and radiant
Stanza III: silken sad
Stanza V: Deep into that darkness

Other examples of *ALLITERATION* in "The Raven"
_____
_____
_____
_____
_____
_____
_____

Name _____

Write A Poe-like Poem

Use the following suggestions for planning a poem of your own, based on techniques you've learned from studying "The Raven."

1. Choose a word or phrase, like *nevermore,* that can be repeated to answer a lot of different questions. Examples are *sometimes*, *I know*, *could be!*, *no*, or *wait and see*. Write the word or phrase that you will repeat in your poem.
_____

2. Decide on a *mood*, or general feeling, for your poem. Will the mood be gloomy? Happy? Mysterious? Funny? Write a word or phrase to describe the mood you wish your poem to create.
_____
_____
_____

3. What Poe Sounds will readers hear in your poem? Jot down some words or phrases you'll experiment with to develop the following:

End rhyme:
_____
_____
_____

Internal rhyme:
_____
_____
_____

Alliteration:
_____
_____
_____

4. Write a draft of your poem on a separate sheet of paper. Then work with a partner to read the poem aloud and revise it.

Eldorado

Synopsis

During the Spanish explorations of the New World in the 16th century, El Dorado was the name given to a legendary land of fabulous wealth that these explorers hoped to find. Through time, El Dorado came to mean finding one's heart's desire. It's this latter meaning that Poe's poem develops: a knight, while young, seeks his goal. Grown old, he still has not reached it. A "pilgrim shadow" tells the knight to keep on looking. The poem's appeal today, even for young people, lies in its message to be brave and constant in the pursuit of one's dream.

Annabel Lee

Synopsis

The speaker's young love, Annabel Lee, dies and is buried by her noble family in a seaside grave. The family had never approved of the love affair, yet even in death they cannot keep the lovers apart—the speaker goes each night to lie down by Annabel Lee's tomb. This poem, like so many others of Poe's works, is based not only on the macabre interest audiences of his time had in premature death, but also on Poe's personal "lost loves." His own wife died very young and very shortly after he had married her. After that, Poe was constantly falling in love with women who were unavailable to him—usually because they were already married.

Teaching Notes

1. Preface your read-alouds by discussing with students the theme of the poem as it's reflected in current media or in books they've read together. Sample start-ups:

• **"Eldorado"** Call on students to name characters in books or TV shows who are looking for an "ideal life." Kids might name Sam, in *My Side of the Mountain*, or Jen, in the TV show *Dawson's Creek*, who is always looking for "good luck." Explain that the knight in "Eldorado" is also looking for perfection.

• **"Annabel Lee"** Ask students to name movies or TV shows that deal with lovers who are separated. Kids may name the modern movie version of *Romeo and Juliet*, starring the hearththrob Leonardo Di Caprio; or the TV show *Buffy the Vampire Slayer*, in which Buffy's boyfriend is carried off to doom, then returns to her. Explain that the speaker in "Annabel Lee" is also focused on a lost love.

2. Distribute the reproducibles on pages 63–66. Read the poems aloud to the class while students follow along.

3. Have students form groups to arrange and practice the poems for reading aloud. On their reproducibles, groups can signify and highlight readers' parts, adapting the format shown for the reading of "The Raven," pages 52–58.

4. Provide practice time for groups, and time for each group to present their rendition to the class. When all groups have read, discuss the similarities and differences in their presentations, and how each one provides a special view of the theme and the characters.

Follow-up

• Distribute the reproducible on page 67. Ask students to use the prompts to plan a film or TV version of one of the poems.
• Continue to refer students to their copies of the Glossary to explore unfamiliar words and to expand their understanding of the poems.

Eldorado
Edgar Allan Poe

I

Gaily bedight,
A gallant knight,
In sunshine and in shadow,
Had journeyed long,
Singing a song,
In search of Eldorado.

II

But he grew old—
This knight so bold—
And o'er his heart a shadow
Fell, as he found
No spot of ground
That looked like Eldorado.

III

And, as his strength
Failed him at length
He met a pilgrim shadow—
"Shadow," said he,
"Where can it be—
This land of Eldorado?"

IV

"Over the Mountains
 Of the Moon,
Down the Valley of the Shadow,
 Ride, boldly ride,"
 The shade replied,—
"If you seek for Eldorado."

Annabel Lee
Edgar Allan Poe

I

It was many and many a year ago,
    In a kingdom by the sea,
That a maiden there lived whom you may know
    By the name of Annabel Lee;—
And this maiden she lived with no other thought
    Than to love and be loved by me.

II

I was a child and *she* was a child,
    In this kingdom by the sea;
But we loved with a love that was more than love—
    I and my Annabel Lee—
With a love that the winged seraphs in Heaven
    Coveted her and me.

III

    And this was the reason that, long ago,
    In this kingdom by the sea,
A wind blew out of a cloud, chilling
    My beautiful Annabel Lee;
So that her high-born kinsmen came
    And bore her away from me,
To shut her up in a sepulchre,
    In this kingdom by the sea.

IV

The angels, not half so happy in Heaven,
    Went envying her and me—
Yes!—that was the reason (as all men know,
    In this kingdom by the sea)
That the wind came out of the cloud by night,
    Chilling and killing my Annabel Lee.

V

But our love it was stronger by far than the love
    Of those who were older than we—
    Of many far wiser than we—
And neither the angels in Heaven above,
    Nor the demons down under the sea,
Can ever dissever my soul from the soul
    Of the beautiful Annabel Lee:—

VI

For the moon never beams, without bringing me dreams
    Of the beautiful Annabel Lee;
And the stars never rise, but I feel the bright eyes
    Of the beautiful Annabel Lee:—
And so, all the night-tide, I lie down by the side
Of my darling—my darling—my life and my bride,
    In her sepulchre there by the sea—
    In her tomb by the sounding sea.

Name _____

Meet You at the Movies

Imagine that you're a movie screenwriter Your task: Plan a film version of either "Eldorado" or "Annabel Lee." Follow these steps:

1. Which poem will you turn into a movie? _____

2. Characters: Name the two main characters, and choose two current movie stars to play the roles.

Main Characters	Actors
A. _____	_____
B. _____	_____

3. Plot: List below some major events that will occur in your film. Because you're stretching a short poem out to make a feature-length film, you'll have to dream up additional events of your own. List the major events in order!

- _____
- _____
- _____
- _____
- _____
- _____

4. Mood and Atmosphere: List some sound effects, music, and descriptions of settings for your movie version of the Poe poem.

- _____
- _____
- _____
- _____
- _____
- _____

5. Share Your Ideas: Work with a partner or group of classmates to revise and finalize your movie plan. Then think of and carry out a way to share your plan with all your classmates.

The Bells

Synopsis

In "The Bells"—as in "The Raven," where the word *nevermore* takes on an increasingly ominous meaning—the sound of bells in this poem moves from cheery to gloomy. The first bells are those on sleighs that carry happy party-goers through the snow. The second bells celebrate a wedding. But the third set of bells signal a fire and foretells disaster; and the fourth bells are those from a church steeple, announcing death and a funeral. What a musical poem! Poe's masterly repetitions and rhythms, his choice of evocative words, and his exquisite rhymes capture the sound and mood of the bells for each event.

Teaching Notes

1. Discuss with students what a bell might signal. Examples: a doorbell (a friend or a stranger?); a school bell (an announcement? an end of a classroom period? a fire drill?); a bell in the community (a holiday? a church service? a fire alarm?). Ask students to follow along on their reproducibles of the poem (pages 70–73), as you read it aloud, to identify the different events signaled by Poe's bells. Discuss the events.

2. After you read the poem aloud, review or introduce the following poetic strategies. Recognizing these strategies will not only help students bring the poem to life as they read it aloud themselves, but also help them write effective poems of their own.

• *Onomatopoeia* (on uh mat uh pee uh) (A word that sounds like the thing designated by the word.) Ask students to find examples of onomatopoeia in lines of "The Bells" and read the words aloud. Examples: in the first stanza, words that capture the sound of merry, frosty bells on a sled in the snow: *tinkle, twinkle, crystalline, jingling*; in the third stanza, words that capture the sound of danger and alarm: *clang, clash; twanging, clanging, jangling, wrangling*.

• *Repetition* The repetition of certain words in Poe's poem captures the repetitive sound of bells—"bells, bells, bells;" "shriek, shriek;" "tolling, tolling, tolling;" time, time, time."

• *Personification* Personification means giving human attributes to nonhuman things. The nonhuman things personified in this poem are the bells themselves. For example, in the first stanza the bells "ring out their delight." By the third stanza, the bells are horrified and screaming. In the final stanza, the bells are ghouls, and the chief bell is a king.

3. Have students read the poem aloud. Students will note that on the reproducible of the poem the four stanzas are arranged for choral reading by four groups. Each group consists of: a solo reader; partners (two students); a choral group (three to five students). (Note: The first and second stanzas are shorter, and the third and fourth stanzas are longer and more challenging by far; you may wish to keep this fact in mind as you help students organize their groups.)

• Ask the class to brainstorm some goals for group practice. For example: reading in unison; coming in on time to keep the flow of the poem going; knowing how to pronounce each word; maintaining the rhythm; reading with expression to capture the mood of the stanza.

• Provide lots of practice time for each group to get its stanza down pat. Act as "roving mentor" to answer questions and to make suggestions.

• Make a first-run tape recording of the class's presentation of "The Bells." Play the tape without comment from you or the class, but ask each group to make notes about how they might improve their performance. After an additional practice session, make and play a second, final tape.

Follow-up

• Distribute the reproducible on page 74. Preview the prompts with the class, then ask students to work independently to write their poems.

• Students can carry out the activities on pages 75–76 and in the Glossary on pages 77–80 to bring together their insights about Poe and his work.

The Bells
Edgar Allan Poe

Teacher   **The Bells**
A Poem by Edgar Allan Poe

I (Group 1)

Solo   Hear the sledges with the bells—
Silver bells!
What a world of merriment their melody foretells!
Partners   How they tinkle, tinkle, tinkle,
In the icy air of night!
While the stars that oversprinkle
All the Heavens, seem to twinkle
With a crystalline delight;
Choral   Keeping time, time, time,
In a sort of Runic rhyme,
To the tintinabulation that so musically wells
From the bells, bells, bells,bells,
Bells, bells, bells—
From the jingling and the tinkling of the bells.

II (Group 2)

Solo   Hear the mellow wedding bells—
Golden bells!
What a world of happiness their harmony foretells!

Partners   Through the balmy air of night
How they ring out their delight!—
From the molten-golden notes
And all in tune,
What a liquid ditty floats
To the turtle-dove that listens while she gloats
On the moon!
Oh, from out the sounding cells
What a gush of euphony voluminously wells!
Chora   How it swells!
How it dwells
On the Future!—how it tells
Of the rapture that impels
To the swinging and the ringing
Of the bells, bells, bells!—
Of the bells, bells, bells, bells,
Bells, bells, bells—
Solo   To the rhyming and the chiming of the bells!

III (Group 3)

Solo   Hear the loud alarum bells—
Brazen bells!
What tale of terror, now, their turbulency tells!
Partners   In the startled ear of Night!
How they scream out their affright!
Too much horrified to speak,
They can only shriek, shriek
Out of tune,
Choral   In a clamorous appealing to the mercy of the fire—
In a mad expostulation with the deaf and frantic fire,
Leaping higher, higher, higher,
With a desperate desire
And a resolute endeavor
Now—now to sit, or never,
By the side of the pale-faced moon.

Partners   Oh, the bells, bells, bells!
             What a tale their terror tells
               Of despair!
             How they clang and clash and roar!
             What a horror they outpour
             In the bosom of the palpitating air!
Choral   Yet the ear, it fully knows,
                By the twanging
                And the clanging
              How the danger ebbs and flows:—
Solo   Yes, the ear distinctly tells,
                In the jangling
                And the wrangling,
             How the danger sinks and swells,
            By the sinking or the swelling in the anger of the bells
              Of the bells—
Choral   Of the bells, bells, bells, bells,
               Bells, bells, bells—
Partners In the clamor and the clangor of the bells.

IV (Group 4)

Solo   Hear the tolling of the bells—
                 Iron bells!
            What a world of solemn thought their monody compels!
Partners   In the silence of the night
               How we shiver with affright
             At the melancholy meaning of the tone!
Solo   For every sound that floats
              From the rust within their throats
                Is a groan.
Partners   And the people—ah, the people
              They that dwell up in the steeple
                 All alone,

              And who tolling, tolling, tolling,
                  In that muffled monotone,
            Feel a glory in so rolling
                  On the human heart a stone—

Choral   They are neither man nor woman—
          They are neither brute nor human,
Solo   They are Ghouls:—
Partners   And their king it is who tolls:—
Choral   And he rolls, rolls, rolls, rolls
                  A Paean from the bells!
            And his merry bosom swells
                  With the Paean of the bells!
            And he dances and he yells;
          Keeping time, time, time,
          In a sort of Runic rhyme,
              To the Paean of the bells—
              Of the bells:—
Partners   Keeping time, time, time,
          In a sort of Runic rhyme,
              To the throbbing of the bells—
        Of the bells, bells, bells—
              To the sobbing of the bells:—
Choral   Keeping time, time, time,
              As he knells, knells, knells,
          In a happy Runic rhyme,
              To the rolling of the bells—
        Of the bells, bells, bells:—
              To the tolling of the bells—
       Of the bells, bells, bells, bells,
          Bells, bells, bells—
Solo   To the moaning and the groaning of the bells.

Name _____

Using Poe's Techniques in Your Poems

1. Try Onomatopoeia

Edgar Allan Poe often chose words that *sound like* the sounds and actions they name. Read the words in each list aloud. Then add more words to the list.

Unhappy, Scary
moan, groan, growl, howl, wail, whimper

_____
_____
_____
_____
_____

Loud, Deep
thunder, thump, rumble, roar, blast, bluster

_____
_____
_____
_____
_____

Quick, Light
clip, snip, rap, tap, skitter, scoot

_____
_____
_____
_____
_____

Breaking
smash, crash, clatter, shatter, slice, slit

_____
_____
_____
_____
_____

2. Try Personification

In "The Bells," Poe uses words that make the bells seem *human*. For example, in stanza four, the bells have "throats." They are "people" who live in the steeple, and they have a "king." Brainstorm for words and phrases that could make the following things seem human.

- Trees in the wind _____
_____

- A fire alarm _____
_____

- A storm at sea _____
_____

3. Write a poem of your own, using onomatopoeia and personification.

Poe's Stories and Poems
Culminating Activities

1. Setting the Poems to Music
Invite students to form small groups, choose one of Poe's poems, and set part or all of it to music, using a guitar, drums, or rhythm instruments, as well as singing voices.

2. Dramatizing and Play Making
- Groups of students can dramatize a Poe poem or one of the stories they've read independently by adapting it for a readers theater presentation.
- Students can work in teams to practice and present pantomimes of a section of a Poe story or poem. Remind students that the pantomime should be vivid and dramatic enough for the audience to accurately guess the specific Poe work on which it is based.
- Invite partners to envision a meeting between two characters in different Poe stories or poems, then dramatize a conversation the two characters might have. Examples: Ligeia and Annabel Lee might discuss what makes them so appealing to the men who love them. Detective Dupin might help the speaker in "The Raven" discover where the gloomy bird has come from.

3. Making and Playing "Poe Games"
In addition to adaptations of the games of Poe-Nopoly and Trivial Poe-Suit described on page 38, students can try these:
- *Finding Poe* Ask the class to form teams and make a list of words that incorporate the letters **p-o-e**. Teams should strive for examples that somehow relate to Poe's stories and poems. Obvious examples are: **poe**try, **poe**m, **poe**t, and onomato**poe**ia. But teams may also think of and list words like sup**po**se, **po**wer, s**po**ke, **pe**ople, and **po**re. Set a time limit for list makers, then ask the teams to list their words on the chalkboard. The winning team is the one that has the most words not used by other teams.

- **Poe Packages** Partners can design, make, and package items that are clues to a specific Poe story or poem. Below are examples for "The Purloined Letter" and "The Masque of the Red Death."

Partner teams exchange boxes, guess the story or poem it represents, and tell how they know. Suggest setting up the packages for a library display or using them as props in a tell-aloud for other students in your school or for visitors from home.

4. Making a Poe Photo Album

Students can make realistic pictures of scenes and characters from Poe's stories and poems, and write a caption for each. Mount the pictures and captions in a large photo album, and leave the album on display for students and classroom visitors to enjoy at their leisure.

Madeline Usher pays a surprise visit.

The "tell-tale heart" made him confess!

Poe's Wonderful Words
An Annotated Glossary

*The words are organized in the order they appear in each poem.
Use the definitions to help you understand the poem.
Try the challenges.*

The Raven

Stanza 1

curious: In Poe's day, this meant *strange*.
   Challenge: Today, *curious* also means:

_____.

lore: knowledge about old beliefs

Stanza 2

wrought (rawt): *made*, as in "a carefully wrought poem"
   Challenge: But *wrought-up* has an entirely diffferent meaning. In "Don't get wrought-up about that," wrought-up means:

_____
_____.

morrow: an old word for "the next day"

surcease (sur-**seeze**): an old word for "end"

Stanza 4

scarce: In Poe's day, a synonym for *hardly*
   Challenges: **1.** Today *scarce* means

_____.

2. In "Make yourself scarce," *scarce* means:

_____.

Stanza 5

token: a mark, sign, or signal
   Challenge: You put a *token* in a slot on the subway. What does this *token* signal or stand for?

_____.

Stanza 6

thereat (ther-**at**): an old word for *there*

Stanza 7

flirt: a quick movement or flutter
   Challenge: Today, *flirt* can also mean

_____.

yore: long ago

obeisance (oh-**bees**-uhns): a deep bow or curtsy

mien (meen): way of acting and looking

bust of Pallas: A *bust* is a sculpture showing head, shoulders, and chest. Pallas was one of the Greek names for Athena, the goddess of arts and wisdom.

Challenge: Why do you think the speaker had a statue of Pallas Athena in his room?

_____
_____.

Stanza 8

beguiling (bee-**gile**-ing): tricking; amusing; entertaining

decorum (dee-**kor**-um): proper behavior

countenance (**cow**-tuh-nunce): facial expression

craven: cowardly

Plutonian shores: Pluto was the god of the Underworld, the dark kingdom where dead souls went. The *shores* were those of the Styx River, which the dead had to cross.

Stanza 9

discourse (dis-**korse**): (verb) to speak or write formally on some important subject

Stanza 11

dirges (**dur**-gis): songs at a funeral

Stanza 12

fancy: (noun) imagination; imaginary pictures.
  Challenge: Today *fancy* can also be an adjective, or describing word. What does *fancy* mean in this sentence:
  She wore a *fancy* dress.

_____.

betook: (verb): Past form of *betake,* an old word that simply means *go*. So, "betook" means *went*.

Stanza 13

divining: predicting, guessing

gloated: In Poe's time, this meant "gazed intently with satisfaction."

Stanza 14

methought (mee-**thot**): past form of the old verb *methinks,* "it seems to me."

censer (**sen**-ser): a container for incense

seraphim (**sehr**-uh-fim): angels

respite (**res**- pit): time or relief and rest

nepenthe (ni-**pen**-thee): in old legends, a drink that caused forgetfulness

quoth (kwoth): an old word for "said"

Stanza 15

balm in Gilead (**gil**-ee-ad): a sweet oil used for annointing the dead and easing their passage into the next world

Stanza 16

Aidenn (**ay**-den): Poe's word for Eden, a happy place
  Challenge: Why did Poe make up a new word? He needed a word to rhyme with

_____.

(Hint: Find it in the line in which *Aidenn* appears.)

Stanza 17

upstarting: rising suddenly

Stanza 18

pallid: pale

seeming (noun): appearance

Eldorado

Stanza 1

gaily: handsomely, beautifully

bedight (bee-**dite**): dressed; equipped.
Challenge: Draw a picture of a "gaily bedight" knight!

Stanza 2

pilgrim shadow: A pilgrim is a wanderer. In Poe's time, *shadow* meant "ghost."
Challenge: In a modern detective story, what does it mean to "shadow" someone?

_____
_____
_____ .
_____ .
_____ .
_____ .

Annabel Lee

Stanza 2

seraphs (**sehr**-ufs): angels

coveted (**kuv**-ut-ed): eagerly desired

Stanza 3

high-born kinsmen: rich, noble family

sepulchre (**sep**-uhl-ker): tomb, grave

Stanza 5

dissever (di-**sev**-ur): separate

The Bells

Stanza 1

crystalline (**krist**-tul-un): icy; made of crystals

runic (**roon**-ik): A rune is a letter of an alphabet used during the Middle Ages. Through the ages, "rune" has come to mean a mark that has a mysterious meaning. Here are the runes that spell Poe:

P   O   E

Challenge: Use a dictionary or encyclopedia to find the runes that spell "Edgar," or your own name!

tintinnabulation (**tin**-tun-nab-you-**lay**-shun): Poe made up this word to capture the sound of ringing bells.

Stanza 2

liquid ditty: As an adjective, *liquid* can mean "flowing and gentle." A *ditty* is a short rhyme.

turtledove: Not a turtle, but a type of dove found in Europe. The turtledove's gentle cooing sound and its affection for its mate has made it a symbol of love and loyalty.

gloats: See "The Raven," stanza 13

sounding cells: *Cells* here means "small rooms," like those in the bell tower from which sounds ring out.

euphony (**yoo**-fuh-nee): a sound that's pleasing to hear

voluminously (vuh-**loo**-muh-nus-lee): greatly, loudly

wells: As a verb, *wells* means "gush" or "pour."

Stanza 3

brazen (**bray**-zn): bold; loud and harsh

turbulency (**tur**-bew-lin-see): confusion, disorder

clamorous (**kla**-more-us): noisy

expostulation (ex-pos-twe-**lay**-shun): a strong protest

bosom: The meaning here is "the very center."

Stanza 4

monody (**mon**-uh-dee): a mournful sound

affright (af-**frite**): a sudden fear

monotone (**mon**-uh-tone): a sound that doesn't change

ghoul (gool): a horrible demon

Paen (**pay**-un): a song of praise

knells (nels): rings slowly and loudly, to warn of a funeral or disaster